P9-BYL-510

GAIL BORDEN
Public Library District
270 No. Grove Avenue
Elgin, Illinois 60120
(847) 742-2411

Special thanks to our adviser:
Susan Kesselring, M.A., Literacy Educator
Rosemount—Apple Valley—Eagan (Minnesota) School District

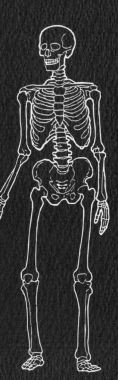

Your **Skin** Weighs **More** Than Your **Brain**

and Other **Freaky Facts** About Your **Skin, Skeleton,** and **Other Body Parts**

by **Barbara Seuling**
illustrated by Matthew Skeens

PICTURE WINDOW BOOKS
Minneapolis, Minnesota

Editor: Christianne Jones
Designer: Abbey Fitzgerald
Page Production: Melissa Kes
Art Director: Nathan Gassman
The illustrations in this book were created digitally.

Picture Window Books
151 Good Counsel Drive
P.O. Box 669
Mankato, MN 56002-0669
877-845-8392
www.picturewindowbooks.com

Text copyright © 2008 by Barbara Seuling
Illustration copyright © 2008 by Picture Window Books

All rights reserved. No part of this book may be
reproduced without written permission from the
publisher. The publisher takes no responsibility for
the use of any of the materials or methods described
in this book, nor for the products thereof.

Printed in the United States of America.

All books published by Picture Window Books
are manufactured with paper containing at least
10 percent post-consumer waste.

Library of Congress Cataloging-in-Publication Data
Seuling, Barbara.
Your skin weighs more than your brain : and other freaky facts
about your skin, skeleton, and other body parts / By Barbara
Seuling ; illustrated by Matthew Skeens.
p. cm.
Includes index.
ISBN: 978-1-4048-3751-5 (library binding)
ISBN: 978-1-4048-3756-0 (paperback)
1. Body, Human—Juvenile literature. I. Skeens, Matthew, ill.
II. Title.
QP37.S4887 2007
612—dc22   2007004030

Table of Contents

A Sound Foundation:
Your Feet and Bones

The size of Americans' feet get larger with each generation.

Not all toes are created equal. Your big toe has only two bones, while the rest have three.

The distance between the inside of your elbow and your wrist is about the same as the length of your foot.

A jogger's feet hit the ground about 2,000 times in 1 mile (1.6 km). When you walk, your feet hit the ground about half of that amount.

Your feet contain 250,000 sweat glands.

The oldest human footprint ever found is 350,000 years old. It was found in volcanic ash in southern Italy.

The foot bones grow faster than any other bones in the body.

Your hands and feet contain more than half of the bones in your body.

A person in bare feet leaves such a strong scent in his or her footprints that it is possible for another person to follow his or her trail.

Tom Dempsey, born in 1947 with only half of a foot, was encouraged by his father to try everything. Tom shares the NFL's record for the longest field goal—63 yards (57 m).

The first Olympic stadium in Greece was based on the size of Hercules' foot. Six hundred of these, a total of 625 feet (191 m), established the length of the stadium.

The standard measurements we use are based on the following: the width of a man's thumb gave us the inch, the length of a man's foot gave us the foot, and the distance between a man's nose and the tip of his middle finger when his arm is outstretched gave us the yard.

The human body has 206 bones.

Bone is very light and full of tiny holes. Your skeleton accounts for only 14 percent of your total body weight.

Bones are so strong that they can cope with twice the squeezing pressure that granite can.

When scientists were looking for a way to protect the heads of football players, researchers studied the woodpecker. The bird hammers steadily with its head without suffering injury. A football helmet was designed with air spaces like those in the woodpecker's skull, which act as shock absorbers.

The only bone that does not connect with any other in the body is the hyoid bone in the throat. It supports the tongue and its surrounding muscles.

The added stress of lots of physical activity causes bones to grow thicker and stronger. On the other hand, lack of physical activity results in bones getting thinner and weaker.

Your skeleton does not hold up your body. It is the muscles and ligaments, not the bones, that hold your body upright.

Your bone cells replace themselves very quickly. This results in a brand new skeleton every seven years.

The hardest part of the human body is not bone. It is tooth enamel.

Your face has 14 bones.

After long space voyages, astronauts show a remarkable loss of bone mass.

By the end of the day, a person has shrunk about 1 inch (2.54 cm)—temporarily. The next morning, a person is back to his or her old height again.

A baby has more bones than an adult. The bones will join together as the baby gets older.

Males and females have different skeletons, including a different elbow angle. Males have slightly thicker and longer legs and arms. Females have a wider pelvis and a larger space within the pelvis.

The smallest bone in the human body is the stirrup bone, located in the middle ear. It is about 0.11 inches (0.28 cm) long.

The strongest bone in your body is your thigh bone, or femur. It is stronger than concrete.

Your femur is the longest bone in your body. It's about one-fourth of your height.

Humans and giraffes have the same number of bones in their necks—seven. Giraffes' neck vertebrae are just much, much longer.

Outer Coverings:

Your Skin, Hair, and Nails

Your skin weighs more than twice as much as your brain.

If you had no skin, your body would dry up like a prune.

Millions of bits of skin flake off your body every day. An average person sheds about 1.5 pounds (0.68 kg) of skin a year.

Dust is made up mostly of dead skin cells.

A scab is clotted blood cells that form a kind of net over a cut. This mass of dried blood cells protects you while new skin is being made. When the new skin is ready, the scab falls off.

During the time of witch trials in Colonial America, birthmarks were considered to be marks made by the devil—a sure sign of a witch.

After the age of 20, a person stops getting new freckles.

You use about 43 muscles to frown. You use just 17 to smile.

It takes 200,000 frowns to produce one wrinkle.

A 3-month-old fetus already has a distinctive set of fingerprints.

Some of the best-preserved mummies in history were about 2,000 years old. They were so well preserved that police were able to take the mummies' fingerprints.

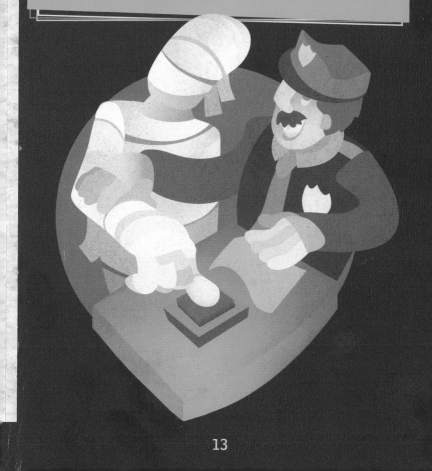

No two sets of fingerprints are alike. Even identical twins have different fingerprints.

Your fingernails are made of the same substance as feathers, claws, beaks, quills, and horns.

Your fingernails grow four times as fast as your toenails.

Of all of your nails, your middle fingernail grows the fastest.

Injured fingernails grow faster than uninjured fingernails.

It takes about six months for a fingernail to grow from the base to the tip.

The white part of your fingernail is called the lunule.

The longest beard ever measured and recorded was that of a Norwegian man, Hans Langseth, born in 1846. His beard was 17.5 feet (5.3 m) long when he died in 1927. It is now in the Smithsonian Institution in Washington, D.C.

Facial hair, such as a beard, grows faster than any other body hair.

Goose bumps are the places where hairs used to be. The body's response to cold is that the hairs stand on end. The hairs create a trap for air, which act as an insulating blanket against the cold. The spaces between the hairs are the goose bumps.

Blonds have more hairs on their heads than brunettes do.

A hair on your head may grow for as long as six years before it falls out.

An average adult has more than 5 million hair follicles. About 100,000 of them are on the head.

Female hair grows more slowly than male hair.

It is normal to lose about 100 hairs a day.

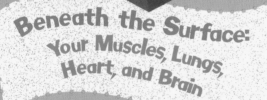

Beneath the Surface: Your Muscles, Lungs, Heart, and Brain

Your heart rests between beats. In an average life of 70 years, your heart will rest for about 40 years.

The heart beats more than 30 million times a year.

You cannot hear a heartbeat. The sound you hear when you listen to someone's heart is that of the valves of the heart closing. The beat itself is a silent contraction, or squeezing, of the muscles.

17

The average body has about 11 pints (5 L) of blood. This blood circulates through the body three times every minute.

Although your heart weighs only about $\frac{1}{200}$ of your body weight, it uses $\frac{1}{20}$ of the blood supply that flows through your body.

Women's hearts beat faster than men's.

The left half of your heart is much stronger and better developed than the right half. That is because the left half has to pump blood through your entire body, while the right half only has to pump blood to the lungs.

Your heart beats about 70 times every minute.

By the time you are 70 years old, your heart will have beaten about 2.5 billion times.

It takes less than 90 seconds for blood to circulate through your entire body.

Placed end to end, the blood vessels in a human would stretch almost three times around the equator. That's about 60,000 miles (96,000 km) of blood vessels.

A single blood cell makes about 3,000 round trips through the circulatory system.

Every second your body manufactures 2.5 million new red blood cells. Within a month, all of your red blood cells are replaced with new ones.

Your stomach can stretch to hold 4 pints (2 L) of fluid.

Your stomach does not really growl. The noises come from a process called borborygmus. It's when the walls of your intestines squeeze together to mix and digest food. Digestion happens when your stomach is full or empty. You just hear it more loudly when there isn't any food in your stomach to muffle the sounds.

Food usually spends at least 10 hours in the large intestine. It can stay there for several days.

Your small intestine is four to five times as long as you are.

It takes seven seconds for food to go from your mouth to your stomach.

The acid in your stomach is so strong that it can dissolve razor blades.

Food stays in your stomach for two to four hours.

Your stomach contains about 35 million digestive glands.

The brain weighs about 3 pounds (1.4 kg).

The brain is 85 percent water.

The brain continues to send out electrical wave signals for about 37 hours after death.

Pain signals travel to the brain more slowly than other touch signals do.

Millions of nerve signals enter your brain every second of your life.

The nervous system sends messages to the brain at speeds of 180 miles (288 km) per hour.

Everyone has a unique pattern of wrinkles on the brain.

Your brain stops growing when you are about 15 years old.

Your brain is more active at night than during the day.

The human body has more than 600 muscles. This is about 40 percent of the body's weight.

You use 200 muscles to take one step. You use 300 to stand still.

It takes 13 muscles in your leg and 20 in your foot to turn your foot outward.

The workout that the average adult gives his or her muscles each day is equal to loading 24,000 pounds (10,800 kg) from the ground onto a 4-foot-high (1.2 m) shelf.

Your tongue is the only muscle attached on just one end.

You use 72 muscles just to speak one word.

The smallest muscle in your body is the stapedius, which is inside the ear.

Your left lung is smaller than your right because it needs to make room for the heart.

The average human inhales 3,500 gallons (13,300 L) of air a day.

Your lungs are so light that they can float on water.

The lungs contain almost 1,500 miles (2,400 km) of airways.

Adult lungs hold an average of 6 pints (2.8 L) of air.

The Amazing Human Machine:
Miscellaneous Body Facts

The highest recorded sneeze speed is more than 100 miles (160 km) per hour.

You can't sneeze with your eyes open.

You're more likely to catch a cold from a person by shaking his or her hand than from his or her sneezing on you.

Laughing and coughing put more pressure on the spine than walking or standing do.

Laughing lowers stress levels and strengthens the immune system, which protects us from getting sick.

A 6-year-old laughs about 300 times a day. An adult laughs about 17 times a day.

Your thumb is the same length as your nose.

A Virginia man was struck by lightening seven times and lived.

A report from a major insurance company shows that baseball players live longer than other people. Among ballplayers, third basemen have the longest lives, and shortstops have the shortest.

The amount of carbon in a human body could make 900 pencils.

There is enough phosphorus in the human body to make more than 2,000 match tips.

You have enough iron in your body to make a 3-inch (7.6-cm) nail.

You have enough fat in your body to make seven bars of soap.

It's impossible to breathe and swallow at the same time.

A runner in a 100-yard (91-m) dash needs about 7 quarts (6.7 L) of oxygen. There is only about 1 quart (0.95 L) of oxygen available in your blood, so fast breathing has to supply the rest.

During your lifetime, your nose and ears never stop growing.

As you get older, you will lose your sense of smell before any of your other senses.

In an average lifespan, most people will walk about 70,000 miles (112,000 km). That's more than three times around the world.

You will spend about one-third of your entire life asleep.

A human being is 75 percent water. That's enough water to fill a 10-gallon (38-L) tank.

In a lifetime, an average person in the United States eats more than 50 tons (45 metric tons) of food.

An average person drinks about 16,000 gallons (60,800 L) of water in a lifetime.

You will urinate 12,000 gallons (45,600 L) in your lifetime. That's enough to fill a small swimming pool.

The human body can survive three minutes without oxygen, three days without water, and three weeks without food.

About one-third of the human population has perfect 20-20 vision.

Your eyesight is the best in the middle of the day.

Women blink twice as much as men.

Your eyes are the same size at birth as they are the rest of your life.

The average human produces 1 quart (0.95 L) of saliva every day. That's about 10,000 gallons (38,000 L) in a lifetime.

Spit is useful. Your teeth grind up what you eat and mix it with spit so that the food can slide down your throat easily.

Your teeth started growing six months before you were born.

The tooth is the only part of the human body that can't repair itself.

One in every 2,000 babies is born with a tooth already showing through the gums.

Every person has a unique tongue print.

Your tongue grows new taste buds about every two weeks.

It is impossible to lick your elbow.

Lack of sleep will kill you sooner than starvation. You can go just 10 days without sleeping, while starvation takes a few weeks.

Your body gives off enough heat in 30 minutes to make a gallon of water boil.

The tallest person ever recorded was 8-foot-11.1-inch (272 cm) Robert Wadlow from Alton, Illinois. He was born on February 22, 1918, and was already 5-feet-4-inches (163 cm) tall at the age of 5.

Rumaisa Rahman is the smallest baby ever born. She weighed just 8.6 ounces (241 grams). That's less than a can of soda.

Scientists have counted more than 500 different liver functions.

Your body needs at least 1,000 calories every day just to survive.

Women burn fat more slowly than men by a rate of about 50 calories a day.

There are more than 30,000 genes inside every cell in your body.

A person living in a hot climate can sweat as much as 3 gallons (11.4 L) a day.

You wash your eyes every time you blink. Your tears wash away germs and kill bacteria.

The average person releases about 1 pint (0.47 L) of gas each day.

Your body contains about 4 ounces (112 grams) of salt.

The reproductive system is the only system that can be removed without threatening life.

Glossary

blood vessels—the narrow tubes that blood flows through

carbon—an element found in all living things and in coal

cell—small, basic unit of living matter

circulatory—your body system that is made up of the heart, blood vessels, blood, and the lymph system

enamel—smooth, hard coating

femur—thigh bone

fetus—an unborn child

follicles—small, ball-shaped groups of cells containing a hole

genes—tiny units of a cell that determine the characteristics that a baby gets from his or her parents

immune system—the system that protects the body from disease

intestine—a long tube that carries and digests food and stores waste products; it is divided into the small intestine and large intestine

ligaments—tough, stretchy bands of tissue

muscle—a tissue in the body that is made of strong fibers; muscles can be tightened or relaxed to make the body move

phosphorus—a substance that looks like white or yellow wax

quills—sharp, needle-like coverings on an animal

saliva—the clear liquid that keeps your mouth moist

skeleton—the structure that supports and protects the body

urinate—to release urine, which is your body's liquid waste

valves—moveable parts in your blood vessels and in your heart that control the flow of blood

vertebrae—small bones that make up the backbone

Index

To Learn More

At the Library
Berger, Melvin. *You're Tall in the Morning but Shorter at Night: And Other Amazing Facts About the Human Body.* New York: Scholastic, 2004.

Brewer, Sarah. *1,001 Facts About the Human Body.* London: DK, 2002.

Seuling, Barbara. *From Head To Toe: The Amazing Human Body and How It Works.* New York: Holiday House, 2002.

Wilkes, Angela. *Question Time: The Human Body.* New York: Kingfisher, 2001.

On the Web
FactHound offers a safe, fun way to find Web sites related to this book. All of the sites on FactHound have been researched by our staff.

1. Visit *www.facthound.com*
2. Type in this special code: 1404837515
3. Click on the FETCH IT button.

Your trusty FactHound will fetch the best sites for you!

Look for all of the books in the Freaky Facts series:

Ancient Coins Were Shaped Like Hams and Other Freaky Facts About Coins, Bills, and Counterfeiting

Cows Sweat Through Their Noses and Other Freaky Facts About Animal Habits, Characteristics, and Homes

Earth Is Like a Giant Magnet and Other Freaky Facts About Planets, Oceans, and Volcanoes

Three Presidents Died on the Fourth of July and Other Freaky Facts About the First 25 Presidents

Your Skin Weighs More Than Your Brain and Other Freaky Facts About Your Skin, Skeleton, and Other Body Parts

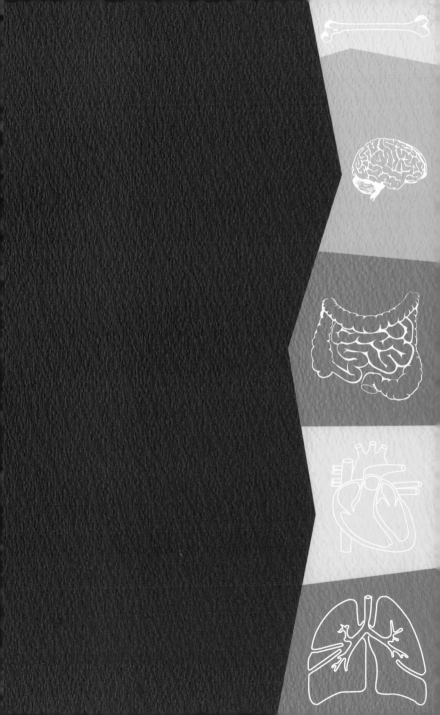